Ultimate Christmas Trees

C.R.Gibson®
FINE GIFTS SINCE 1870

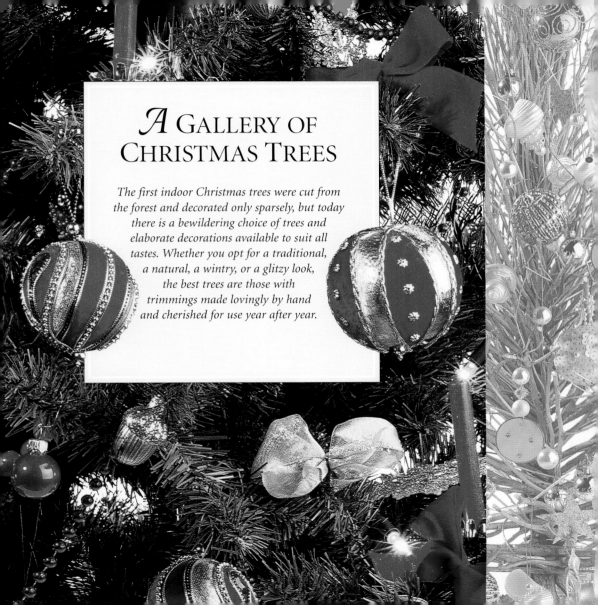

A GALLERY OF CHRISTMAS TREES

*The first indoor Christmas trees were cut from
the forest and decorated only sparsely, but today
there is a bewildering choice of trees and
elaborate decorations available to suit all
tastes. Whether you opt for a traditional,
a natural, a wintry, or a glitzy look,
the best trees are those with
trimmings made lovingly by hand
and cherished for use year after year.*

SELECTING TREES & CONTAINERS

WITH SO MANY CHRISTMAS TREES available, we can have whatever we want – will you enjoy the evocative scent of a cut or potted fresh tree, the convenience of an artificial tree, or something modern, stylish, and completely different? The answer depends on your purposes; it helps to consider cost, available space, and how long the tree needs to last. Once the tree is chosen, select a container to match.

BLUE SPRUCE
(See also page 9)
This prickly tree takes its name from its exceptional blue tinge, which looks fabulous with red and gold decorations. It retains its large needles quite well, but those that fall can be painful to step on.

REAL TREES

Choose a potted tree with roots if you wish to replant it after Christmas. Alternatively, a cut tree can retain its needles quite well if placed in water.

Small, glossy leaves

Characteristic spiky, blue-green needles

BAY TREE (See also page 34)
This small leafy tree with a neat round shape is unusual, but ideal for a small room. Keep it in a pot, water it regularly, and dress it with scaled-down decorations for Christmas. If you prefer, bays are available from garden centers, clipped in the classic pine tree shape.

Variegated leaves add color to the tree

HOLLY TREE (See also page 18)
Instead of using just a few sprigs of festive holly, why not bring the whole tree indoors for Christmas? Choose a holly tree in glossy green with red berries, a cultivar on a long stem, or an interesting variety with variegated leaves.

Pretty cane container hides a functional watertight pot

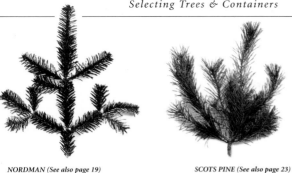

Containers

Place rooted trees in watertight containers filled with damp soil, and put cut trees in water, soil, or sand.

Steel bucket, practical for a real tree, is easily filled with soil or water.

NORDMAN (See also page 19)
A soft and bushy fir tree that tends to retain its glossy green needles, making it ideal to cut and keep indoors. The layered branches are easy to decorate.

SCOTS PINE (See also page 23)
This popular tree should retain its needles throughout the Christmas period. Take care when hanging glass baubles on the ends of the soft branches; they can easily slip off.

Decorated terracotta pot must be glazed if filled with damp soil.

Branch can be seen beneath the sparse green needles

Terracotta pot is ideal for all trees, and is inexpensive and easy to paint.

NORWEGIAN SPRUCE (See also page 35)
Choose this green tree for its full and bushy shape, tapering to a single stem at the top. Needles are prickly and sparse, showing the bronze of the branches beneath.

Decorated wicker container hides a watertight pot

Copper bucket suits the colors of real trees rather than artificial ones.

ARTIFICIAL TREES

A high-quality artificial tree can be used for years.
If storage space is at a premium, opt for one that can
be dismantled. Styles are not limited to fir trees –
imaginative alternatives are available to suit all tastes.

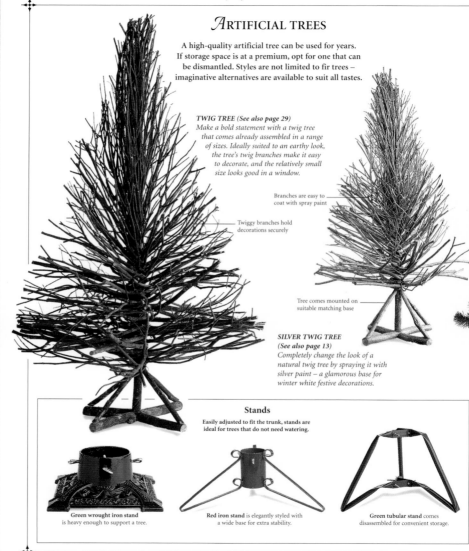

TWIG TREE (See also page 29)
*Make a bold statement with a twig tree
that comes already assembled in a range
of sizes. Ideally suited to an earthy look,
the tree's twig branches make it easy
to decorate, and the relatively small
size looks good in a window.*

Branches are easy to
coat with spray paint

Twiggy branches hold
decorations securely

Tree comes mounted on
suitable matching base

**SILVER TWIG TREE
(See also page 13)**
*Completely change the look of a
natural twig tree by spraying it with
silver paint – a glamorous base for
winter white festive decorations.*

Stands

Easily adjusted to fit the trunk, stands are
ideal for trees that do not need watering.

Green wrought iron stand
is heavy enough to support a tree.

Red iron stand is elegantly styled with
a wide base for extra stability.

Green tubular stand comes
disassembled for convenient storage.

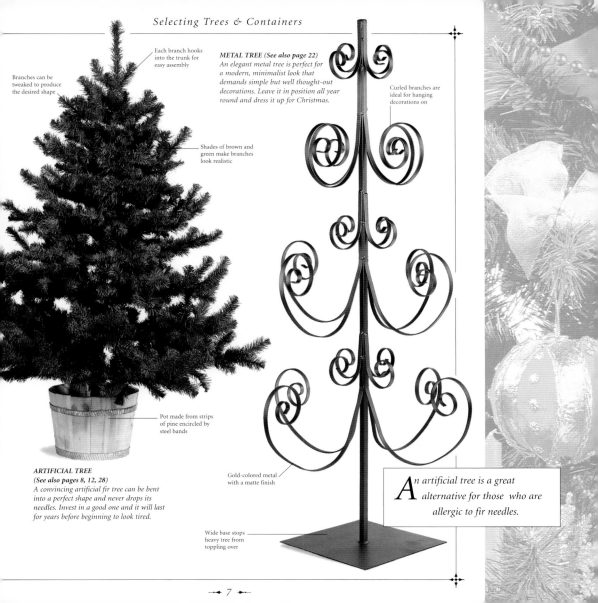

Branches can be tweaked to produce the desired shape

Each branch hooks into the trunk for easy assembly

METAL TREE (See also page 22)
An elegant metal tree is perfect for a modern, minimalist look that demands simple but well thought-out decorations. Leave it in position all year round and dress it up for Christmas.

Curled branches are ideal for hanging decorations on

Shades of brown and green make branches look realistic

Pot made from strips of pine encircled by steel bands

Gold-colored metal with a matte finish

ARTIFICIAL TREE
(See also pages 8, 12, 28)
A convincing artificial fir tree can be bent into a perfect shape and never drops its needles. Invest in a good one and it will last for years before beginning to look tired.

Wide base stops heavy tree from toppling over

*A*n artificial tree is a great alternative for those who are allergic to fir needles.

TRADITIONAL TREES

REGAL RED AND GOLD are used to give these classic trees a traditional festive look, mixing old-fashioned and handmade decorations with modern, store-bought baubles. Wired bows, cranberry rings, and craft dough shapes jostle for pride of place with glitzy gold tassels and garlands of ruby red beads, while wax candles add a timeless quality.

ANTIQUE LOOK
Smother an artificial tree with a thousand and one red and gold decorations, from heirlooms passed down the generations to new classic baubles with a twist. Lighting wax candles on the tree is not recommended, so use white Christmas lights for sparkle.

Cranberry ring shines among the baubles

Begin by winding white Christmas lights around the tree

Garland of red beads spirals down the tree

Glossy glass balls fill in gaps

Position large velvet baubles where they will catch the light

Add tiny baskets of candy on lower branches

Velvet cheat's bow

Red-painted terracotta pot adorned with large bow and tassel

WE THREE KINGS
Choose a traditional crimson and gold theme to complement a beautiful blue spruce tree, using golden camels, opulent eastern crowns, and sparkling strings of stars to tell the Christmas story. Finish with scarlet berries, thick shining tassels, gold snowflakes, and iridescent baubles.

A *Christmas tree is a public display of one's personal taste and private celebration.*

Bunch of holly berries

Weave a garland of gold stars among the branches

Gilded craft dough camel (see page 10)

Jeweled crowns (see page 11)

Scatter oversized tassels randomly on the branches

Mirrored stars

Terracotta pot contains damp soil to keep tree fresh

MAKING THE CRAFT DOUGH CAMELS

One recipe of dough will make about ten camels, but if you need fewer, unbaked dough will last for several weeks wrapped in plastic wrap and kept in the refrigerator. Painting the shapes with a coat of varnish gives extra protection and shine.

• EQUIPMENT •

Pencil
Cardboard
Scissors
Cutting mat
Mixing bowl
Wooden spoon
Water
Flour, to dust
Rolling pin
Kitchen knife
Garlic press
Baking tray
Pin
Wire rack
Paintbrush
Varnish (optional)
Glue

Ingredients

2 cups flour

1 cup salt

Gold paint

6in (15cm) cord

Red paint

30 tiny beads

1 Draw a camel on a piece of cardboard and cut it out carefully with a craft knife.

2 Mix the flour and salt in a bowl, then gradually stir in 1 cup of water to make a dry but workable mixture.

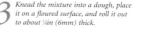

3 Knead the mixture into a dough, place it on a floured surface, and roll it out to about ¼in (6mm) thick.

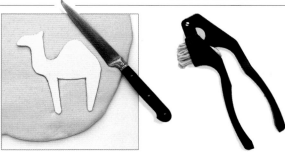

4 Place the template on the dough and cut around it with a sharp knife. Repeat to make a total of ten camels.

5 Cut and engrave a little piece of dough to make a saddle for each camel, and push more dough through a garlic press to make a fringe for the saddle. Position these details on the camels ready for baking.

6 Place the camels on a baking tray and bake on the lowest setting for about 4 hours, or until the dough is hard but not brown. Prick the back of the camel with a pin to test for firmness. Cool on a wire rack.

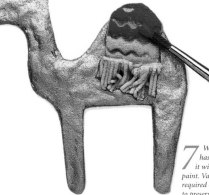

*F*or the adventurous, tradition begins anew each year.

7 When the camel has cooled, decorate it with red and gold paint. Varnish it if required – this will help to preserve the camel.

Jeweled Crowns

Use the same method to make craft dough crowns that hang from the tree on loops of gold cord. Add intricate details, paint them red and gold, and decorate with sparkly gold beads. Glue a loop of cord to the back to finish.

8 Loop a piece of gold cord and glue it to the back for hanging. Glue tiny beads to the saddle to finish.

White Trees

These glittering trees topped with silver stars sparkle like winter frost in the early morning sun. The delicate branches are laden with decorations made from frosted glass, translucent mother-of-pearl, masses of shimmering sequins, gleaming silver ribbon, and shells wrapped in decadent lengths of pearlized beads. The effect is pure Christmas magic.

SNOW WHITE
Wind Christmas lights and a shimmering silver ribbon in and out of the branches, working from the top down. Intersperse large white frosted baubles with shiny hearts, and add smaller silver balls in mirrored and etched glass to finish.

Artificial tree suits white and silver decorations

Use white Christmas lights to highlight your favorite baubles

Large frosted bauble

Twist silver wire-edged ribbon around the tree

Terracotta pot sprayed silver and edged with a garland of silver beads

Top the tree with
a glittery star and
frosted glass grapes

FROSTED TWIG TREE
*Spray a twig tree silver and contrast
sparkling silver baubles with creamy
sequin-covered globes. Fill empty branches
with lustrous polished shells on silver braid,
small gleaming glass baubles, and chandelier
droplets reminiscent of slippery icicles.*

Decorated shell
(see page 17)

Use small baubles
to fill in gaps

Hang large sequin
baubles (see page 16)
on the tree first

Brass-edged
mother-of-pearl disc

*W hite trees add a bit of
wintry charm to the holidays
for those who live in a warm climate.*

Bauble suspended
from rope of
pearly beads

Twig tree comes
with its own stand

PEARLY DECORATIONS

IN THE MONTHS BEFORE CHRISTMAS, start collecting sequins in shades of silver and cream, old pearl bead necklaces, fancy braid, shiny silver ribbons, and highly polished seashells to turn into gleaming decorations. Buy foam balls from craft stores and mix their round shapes with the elegance of long chandelier droplets for a stunning winter white Christmas tree.

SEQUIN BAUBLE Ingredients

• EQUIPMENT •

Darning needle

Glue

Foam ball, 8in (20cm) in circumference

8in (20cm) bead trim

200 pearly sequins

50 silver sequins

250 pins

4in (10cm) silver cord

Sequin bauble (see page 16)

String of beads used to suspend bauble

DECORATED SHELL Ingredients

2¾in (7cm) polished shell

8in (20cm) string pearl beads

2 small pearl beads

4in (10cm) silver cord

• EQUIPMENT •

Glue

IRIDESCENT SEQUIN BAUBLE
Pin masses of gleaming sequins to a large cotton ball and add a smattering of round pearl beads to decorate.

Chandelier droplet hanging from decorated shell

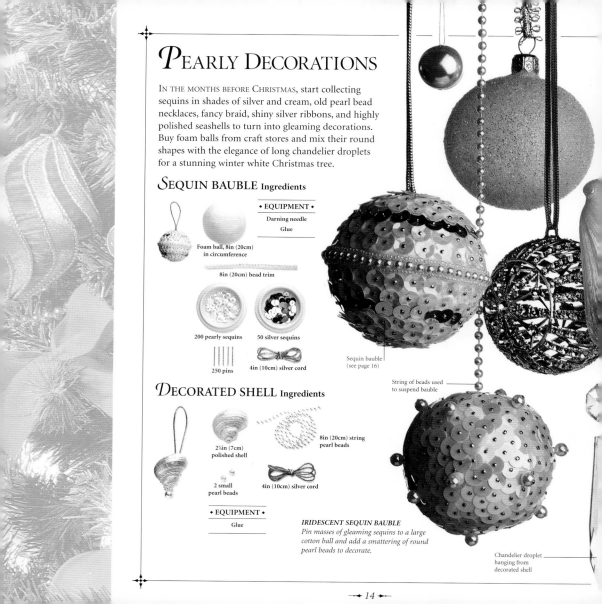

Mirrored
bauble
reflects
the light

Wire-edged
organza ribbon

BAUBLE AND BOW
*Tie silver wire-edged
ribbon in a bow on
top of a small pearly
bauble decorated with
dots of glitter.*

Abalone shell
with natural
holes, from
a shell shop

Polished shell
wrapped with
beads (see page 17)

ICICLE PENDANTS
*Contrast an opaque patterned
glass bauble on silver braid
with graceful glass droplets.*

SHINING SHELLS
*Look in shell shops for
shells polished until the
underlying mother-of-
pearl shows through.*

Silver sequin bauble
(see page 16)

MAKING THE SEQUIN BAUBLE

Stick to one or two simple colors of sequins, or experiment with alternating bands in vibrant colors. Wrapping strings of jazzy beads around the bauble adds glamor. WARNING: pinned sequin baubles can be dangerous for young children and animals.

1 Glue the bead trim horizontally around the center of the foam ball, making sure the trim is straight.

2 Working upward from the bead trim, push pins one by one through the center of the pearly sequins to secure them to the foam ball in two neat, slightly overlapping rings.

4 Continue pinning on rings of pearl sequins until you reach the top of the ball, but leave space to make a hole. Repeat steps 2 through 4, working down from the bead trim.

3 After two rings of pearly sequins, add a row of silver sequins using the same technique.

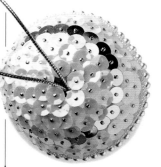

5 Make a hole in the top of the ball with a darning needle and squeeze some glue into it. Make a loop of silver cord and push the ends into the hole to finish.

Pearls and Sequins

Studded Pearl Bauble
Cover a foam ball completely with pearl sequins, then pin a few pearl beads on top of the sequins. Hang from a string of pearls.

Silver Sequin Bauble
Divide a foam ball into quarters with four lines of pearl beads pinned in position, then fill in the quarters with silver sequins.

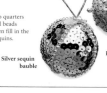

Silver sequin bauble

Studded pearl bauble

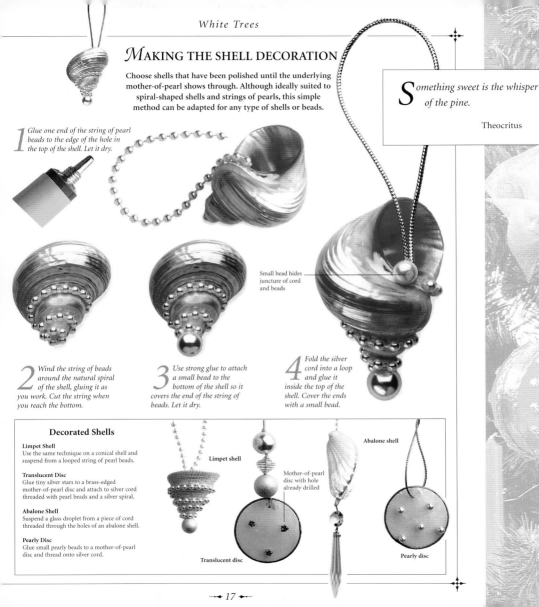

MAKING THE SHELL DECORATION

Choose shells that have been polished until the underlying mother-of-pearl shows through. Although ideally suited to spiral-shaped shells and strings of pearls, this simple method can be adapted for any type of shells or beads.

*S*omething sweet is the whisper of the pine.

Theocritus

1 Glue one end of the string of pearl beads to the edge of the hole in the top of the shell. Let it dry.

Small bead hides juncture of cord and beads

2 Wind the string of beads around the natural spiral of the shell, gluing it as you work. Cut the string when you reach the bottom.

3 Use strong glue to attach a small bead to the bottom of the shell so it covers the end of the string of beads. Let it dry.

4 Fold the silver cord into a loop and glue it inside the top of the shell. Cover the ends with a small bead.

Decorated Shells

Limpet Shell
Use the same technique on a conical shell and suspend from a looped string of pearl beads.

Translucent Disc
Glue tiny silver stars to a brass-edged mother-of-pearl disc and attach to silver cord threaded with pearl beads and a silver spiral.

Abalone Shell
Suspend a glass droplet from a piece of cord threaded through the holes of an abalone shell.

Pearly Disc
Glue small pearly beads to a mother-of-pearl disc and thread onto silver cord.

Limpet shell

Mother-of-pearl disc with hole already drilled

Abalone shell

Translucent disc

Pearly disc

COUNTRY-STYLE TREES

REJOICE IN ALL THINGS NATURAL at Christmastime, decking your tree out with flower petals, rich spices, ornate carved fruit, raffia baubles, and rosebuds, all bathed in the natural glow of candlelight. For something completely different, suspend golden pears from a variegated holly tree, and perch a fat gold partridge in a raffia nest among the branches.

PARTRIDGE IN A PEAR TREE
For a quirky take on the well-known Christmas carol, perch a golden partridge in a red raffia nest among the branches of a traditional holly tree. Golden pears hanging from the lowest branches complete the look.

Variegated holly, clipped into shape

Chicken wire scrunched into shape and sprayed gold

Cardboard pear covered in gold leaf

FRUIT, SPICE, AND ALL THINGS NICE
Fill the room with fragrance by gluing aromatic spices, such as star anise, and small chilies to foam balls, and by using dried oranges, rose petals, and bunches of oregano as decorations. Echo the deep green of a Nordman fir with soft green candles and complete the earthy theme with a woven cane basket.

Wooden animal shape covered in a light dusting of chalk

Green wax candles for decoration

Dried orange bauble (see page 21)

String bauble echoes the natural theme

Flower ball (see page 20)

*H*andmade decorations take less time and are more fun to create than driving to the mall, fighting the crowds, and selecting a box of ornaments no one else wanted.

MAKING THE FLOWER BALL

Dried roses are ideal for making flower balls because the petals are slightly flexible and quite flat and retain much of their color when dried. Carefully open the petals and glue them so the best side faces outward.

Ingredients

Medium-gauge floral wire

♦ EQUIPMENT ♦

Darning needle

Glue

10 dried roses per ball

Foam ball, 8in (20cm) in circumference

Slightly overlap each ring of petals to hide the yellow tops

1   Gently pull the petals from the roses, making sure they are not damaged in the process. Discard imperfect petals.

2   Starting at the bottom of the ball, glue the petals on one by one so they form a slightly overlapping ring.

3   Continue gluing the petals on, working around the ball toward the top, creating neat rings of petals.

4   When the ball is completely covered, use a darning needle to make a hole in the top. Fill it with glue and push in a piece of floral wire. To finish, bend the wire into a hook for hanging.

Spicy Balls

Use the same technique to make baubles covered with tiny dried chilies, adzuki beans, or dried star anise, which fills the room with a lovely aroma.

Dried chilies

Adzuki beans

Dried star anise

Making the Citrus Baubles

The thick skin of oranges lends itself well to carving, so
practice on them before attempting the thinner skin of limes.
For perfectly dried baubles, choose very fresh, unwaxed
produce and leave somewhere warm and dry for about two weeks.

Ingredients

Thick-gauge floral wires

Fresh, unwaxed citrus fruit

◆ EQUIPMENT ◆

Canelle knife

Darning needle

Glue

*1 Use a canelle knife to start carving
a spiral pattern into the skin of a
plump, round, unwaxed orange.*

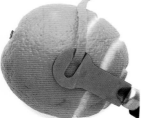

*2 Slowly continue the spiral until it
reaches the bottom of the orange. If
the peel breaks, start again from that
point. Carve different patterns into other
fruit (see inset) to make an entire set.*

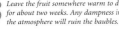
Ready to dry   **Dried**

*3 Leave the fruit somewhere warm to dry
for about two weeks. Any dampness in
the atmosphere will ruin the baubles.*

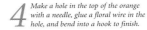

*4 Make a hole in the top of the orange
with a needle, glue a floral wire in the
hole, and bend into a hook to finish.*

GLITZY TREES

DIFFERENT TONES OF BLUE set off the burnished gold of a metal tree, and bright fuchsia contrasts with the dense green of a thick pine tree for a vivid festive look that is utterly glamorous. Homemade decorations in rich fabrics are mixed with vibrant glass baubles and hung from glossy satin cord, and the trees are given added sparkle by Christmas lights or wax candles.

STYLISHLY MODERN
Team a metal tree with gleaming glass and satin baubles and chunky wax candles for a restrained but striking glitzy look. Match items on each side of the tree to reflect its elegant symmetry, and graduate color from the bottom to the top to carry the eye upward.

Bias-cut checked silk bauble (see page 27)

Three-tiered bauble (see page 26)

Contrast chunky wax candles in shades of blue and green with the round baubles

Bauble cord held in position with sticky tape

Deep turquoise string bauble with tassel

PINK, PURPLE, AND GOLD
Load a Scots pine tree with dazzling colored glass baubles, raw silk pouches, shiny foil crackers, and tiny wrapped gifts nestling in the branches. Scatter golden garlands throughout; add multicolored Christmas lights and place a theatrical star on top to steal the limelight.

Christmas light shines on the gold star

Shiny silk string baubles dotted randomly on tree

Tiny gift wrapped in shiny paper

Rest tiny foil crackers on the bushy branches

Pouch made from luxurious silk saturated in color

Layer of moss covers damp soil

Mauve-blue basket tied with cerise ribbon

O Christmas tree, O Christmas tree,
How lovely are your branches.
In summer sun, in winter snow,
A dress of green you always show,
O Christmas tree, O Christmas tree,
How lovely are your branches.

German Carol

FABRIC BAUBLES

WIND SHIMMERING FABRICS AND TRIMMINGS in jewel-like colors around lightweight foam balls to make sumptuous tree decorations and add textural contrast to the extravagant display with store-bought glass and spangled baubles. Break up their strong outlines with iridescent ribbons twisted into bows, and suspend your opulent creations from lengths of colored tinsel ribbon and glittering braid, silk yarn, and gold cord.

THREE-TIERED BAUBLE Ingredients

Foam ball, 8in (20cm) in circumference

Foam ball, 4in (10cm) in circumference

5½yd (5m) knitting yarn

Three colored knitting yarns, 8½yd (8m) each

Foam ball, 3in (8cm) in circumference

• EQUIPMENT •

Tweezers

Darning needle

Fabric glue

½yd (0.5m) thick gold rope

3¼yd (3m) thin twisted gold cord

5½yd (5m) knitting yarn

GOLD GLITTER BALL
Soften the effect of a store-bought gold bauble with a delicate gold and turquoise voile bow.

CHECKED SILK BAUBLE Ingredients

½yd (0.5m) gold cord

Glittering theatrical tassel

• EQUIPMENT •

Dressmaking pins

Fabric scissors

Iron

Fabric glue

Silk, ½ x ½yd (0.5 x 0.5m)

T-pin

Foam ball, 8in (20cm) in circumference

Store-bought gold tassel

CHECKED SILK BAUBLE
Wrap thin strips of gleaming checked silk haphazardly around a ball for a rich, vibrant effect. An oversized gold tassel provides a bold splash of glitter.

GLASS BAUBLES
Combine metallic glass baubles with fabric decorations.

JADE BALL
Set jade dupion silk against an elegant green voile bow.

Sparking gold cord connects each ball

THREE-TIERED BAUBLE
Wrap silky blue, purple, and multicolored yarns around three balls. Use gold cord to highlight the colored segments and lead the eye through the decoration.

PLUM BALL
Wind vivid purple yarn onto a ball and enhance it with a wire-edged bow and gold braid.

GREEN AND PURPLE BAUBLE
Thread emerald green and deep purple knitting yarns through a foam ball to create solid blocks of color edged with gold braid. Secure blue tinsel ribbon to the bauble with a T-pin.

MAKING THE THREE-TIERED BAUBLE

First make a hole in the large foam ball (see inset below). Then divide each of the three 8½yd (8m) lengths of yarn into quarters before threading them through the hole. Yarns are wound onto the small balls and glued.

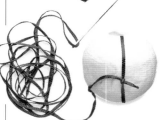  

1 Thread one piece of blue yarn on a needle, pass it through the hole in the large ball, and tie it to form a loop.

2 Twist the knot into the hole to conceal it and continue threading the yarn through the ball, as shown, creating a segment of color. Secure the end by hooking it under previous turns of yarn.

3 Repeat with one piece of purple yarn, then one piece of multicolored yarn. Alternate the colors until the ball is covered. Then thread 3yd (2.75m) of thin gold cord around each segment. Secure as before.

5 With a darning needle, pull the rest of the gold cord through the smaller balls. Between each two balls, make a knot and leave 1in (2.5cm) of cord. Glue the cord into the hole at the bottom of the large ball.

Secure the
loose end of
yarn with glue

4 Wind a length of purple yarn around the small ball and a length of blue yarn around the medium ball.

Leave 1in (2.5cm) of gold
cord between each ball

Making a hole in a ball

Using a darning needle, carefully make a tiny hole in a foam ball. Gradually increase the width of the hole with a small knife. Then work from the other end of the ball in the same way until the hole is about 1in (2.5cm) wide all through the ball.

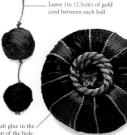

Dab glue in the
top of the hole

6 Glue a 2½in (6cm) piece of gold rope around the top of the hole in the large ball. Knot one end of the remaining rope and glue it into the hole. Tie the other end of the rope to the tree.

MAKING THE CHECKED SILK BAUBLE

Start by cutting the silk on the bias (see inset steps below),
to create thin strips that mold themselves easily around
the circular foam shape. The number of strips you use
depends on how you wrap them on the ball.

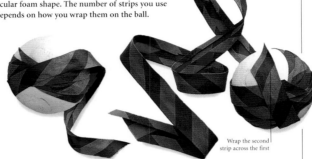

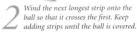

Wrap the second
strip across the first

Cutting strips on the bias

1 Fold the square of silk diagonally in half to locate the longest bias line. Place pins along this folded edge at ½in (1cm) intervals.

2 Open up the square and cut along the bias, removing the pins as you go. Continue to cut each half of silk into 1½in (3.5cm) wide strips.

3 Turn the raw edges of the strips over and pin to the wrong side of the silk. Press them with an iron, removing the pins, to create a neat finish.

1 Wrap the longest strip of silk around the ball, securing the end by overlapping it with the next turn of fabric.

Push the T-pin through the end of silk

2 Wind the next longest strip onto the ball so that it crosses the first. Keep adding strips until the ball is covered.

3 Secure the last strip with a T-pin. Hook a loop of gold cord with knotted ends under the pin for hanging.

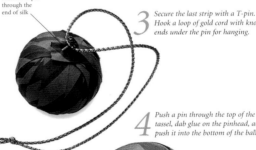

4 Push a pin through the top of the tassel, dab glue on the pinhead, and push it into the bottom of the ball.

EDIBLE TREES

A CHRISTMAS TREE CREAKING under the weight of delicious-looking edible decorations is a delight to the eye as well as the palate. Choose a natural color scheme using cookies and dried fruit, or pander to the children of the house with a tempting mix of colored candies, lollipops, wrapped chocolates, and net bags of gold-wrapped chocolate coins.

CONFECTIONERY DELIGHT
For a tree that is a guaranteed hit with children, twist wire around the ends of wrapped candies to make long garlands, and bundle small candies into squares of cellophane tied with colorful cord. Attach brightly wrapped candies and lollipops with pieces of wire and set the whole tree ablaze with red Christmas lights.

Candy cane hooked over branch

Colored candies in cellophane packets

Garland of wrapped chocolates twisted on wire

Quirky vegetable-shaped baubles

Tie long pieces of marshmallow to the tree with ribbon

Sacks of gold coins placed randomly

Red checked bow
tied at top of tree

Begin by twisting
garlands around
the tree

Use tiny wicker
baskets to fill gaps

Cranberry and
kumquat garland
(see page 33)

FRUIT AND BERRIES
*Make garlands from dried fruit, miniature
marshmallows, and cranberries on wire
or thread and fill tiny wicker baskets with
scented cloves or chopped nuts. Fly decorated
gingerbread angels (see page 32) from the
branches and bake an extra plate without
embellishment to eat.*

Add large gingerbread
angels (see page 32) when
the garlands are in position

Cranberry and
apricot garland

*D ecorations that seem good
enough to eat may end up in
tiny hands and mouths if care is not
taken to place them out of reach.*

EDIBLE TREE DECORATIONS

FOR DECORATIVE FESTIVE garlands, thread shiny cranberries and kumquats studded with aromatic cloves onto wire, or alternate dried cherries, apricot slices, and miniature marshmallows. Suspend gingerbread angels with golden wings from gold rings trimmed with ribbon, and bake an unadorned batch for eating (one recipe makes ten angels).

GINGERBREAD ANGEL Ingredients

Gingerbread dough

Pad of gold leaf (optional)

SAFETY FIRST
Do not eat angels with rings glued to them; bake a separate plate for eating.

White of egg, optional

10 curtain rings

59in (150cm) gold thread

◆ EQUIPMENT ◆	
Paper	Wire rack
Pencil	Bowl (optional)
Scissors	Egg whisk (optional)
Flour, to dust	
Rolling pin	Fine paintbrush (optional)
Kitchen knife	
Nonstick baking parchment	Spoon
Baking tray	Glue

1yd (1m) checked ribbon

CRANBERRY GARLAND Ingredients

5 kumquats

50 cloves

◆ EQUIPMENT ◆
Wire cutters

70 cranberries per 1yd (1m) wire

Medium-gauge floral wire

Wicker basket filled with cloves

NATURAL COLORS
Give decorations a natural feel using the muted colors of dried fruit, cloves, wicker baskets, gingerbread, and gingham ribbon, and brighten the effect with fresh kumquats.

Marshmallows and
cranberries strung
in a garland

Marshmallows,
threaded with
alternating dried
apricot slices and
dried cherries

Flying angel

Cranberries and
dried apricot slices

Cranberry garland adorned
with kumquats (see page 33)

MAKING THE GINGERBREAD ANGELS

Make up sufficient gingerbread to create ten angels.
If you do not wish to use gold leaf, decorate with colored icing
or gold paste from a cake-decorating store instead.

*1 Make an angel template, copy it
onto paper and cut it out. Mix the
gingerbread dough and roll it out
on a lightly floured surface to a thickness
of about ¼in (6mm).*

Reroll the dough to
get ten neat angels

*2 Place the paper angel on the dough
and cut around it with a small kitchen
knife. Repeat to make ten angels.*

*3 Line a baking tray with nonstick
kitchen parchment and lay the
gingerbread angels carefully on
it. Bake at 375°F/190°C for 8–10 minutes,
until firm. Cool on a wire rack.*

*4 If using gold leaf, lightly whisk the
white of an egg and paint it onto the
angel's wings with a fine paintbrush.
Otherwise decorate the angel as desired and
add the ring and bow as directed in step 6.*

Gold leaf applied by rubbing with back of spoon

5 Tear a sheet of gold leaf and its backing from a pad. Cut a piece the size of the angel's wing and position it on the wing. Rub the backing with the back of a spoon to apply the transfer.

6 Peel the backing off and repeat with the other wing. To finish, glue a gold ring to the back of the angel's head. Tie a small bow to the top of the curtain ring with gold thread and hang from a long loop of gold thread.

MAKING THE CRANBERRY GARLAND

Fresh red cranberries interspersed with kumquats make ideal decorative garlands and remain attractive when dried. Miniature marshmallows, dried fruit slices, cherries, and figs strung on thread make delicious edible garlands.

1 Push the cloves one by one into the kumquats to form a ring around the middle of each fruit.

2 Thread the cranberries onto a reel of wire, adding a studded kumquat after nine or ten cranberries.

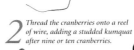

3 Continue threading cranberries and kumquats until the garland is the desired length. To finish, bend large loops in the ends of the wire to prevent the fruit from sliding off the ends.

CARNIVAL TREES

HOT, RIOTOUS COLORS bring instant warmth and sunshine indoors for Christmas. Golden suns, vibrant tinplate shapes, dazzling baubles, and long garlands of paper beads almost hide the branches of a Norwegian spruce, and vividly colored miniature citrus fruits nestle among the glossy green leaves of a bay tree.

TIE A YELLOW RIBBON
Wire tiny citrus-colored bows to kumquats and small limes and scatter them evenly throughout the leaves of a bushy bay tree. Match the bows with a lemon yellow ribbon spiraled around the trunk.

Cheat's bow attached to small lime and fixed to branch with wire

Thick yellow ribbon wound around trunk

FESTIVE FUN
*Crowd a Norwegian spruce with
masses of paper, tin, and glass decorations
in the craziest colors possible. Fill spaces
with jazzy baubles, snake a garland of
paper beads through the branches,
and add multicolored Christmas
lights to finish.*

Tinplate fish
(see page 36)

Aztec-style sun

Multicolored
paper bead garland
(see page 37)

*T*radition holds that the first
Christmas tree was conceived by
the great reformer Martin Luther who
wanted to capture the beauty of
sparkling snow framed in the
moonlight against a fir tree and bring
it into his home for everyone to enjoy.

MAKING THE TINPLATE FISH

Check your telephone directory for suppliers of sheets of
tinplate and choose a thin sheet that is easy to cut.
To avoid damaging the table top when punching patterns
into tinplate, use a piece of thick cardboard as a base.

◆ EQUIPMENT ◆

Sharp pencil
Cardboard
Craft knife
Cutting mat
Old scissors
Thick card
Nail
Hammer
Hole punch

Ingredients

Tinplate, 6½ x 2⅜in (16 x 6cm)

Felt-tip pens

6in (15cm) cord

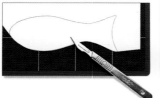

1 Make a fish template, copy it
onto a piece of cardboard; cut it out
carefully with a scalpel.

2 Place the cardboard template on the
sheet of tinplate and score around it
with a sharp pencil.

3 Use old, blunt scissors to cut
carefully around the scored line,
making sure there are no jagged edges.

Tap the nail
gently to avoid
piercing the tin

4 Place the tinplate fish on a piece of thick
cardboard; use a nail and hammer to
punch a pattern on the shiny side.

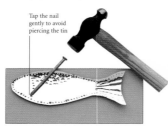

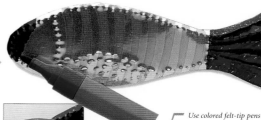

5 Use colored felt-tip pens
to decorate the shiny side
of the fish. Pierce one end
with a hole punch and thread a
piece of cord through it to hang
(see inset).

MAKING THE PAPER BEAD GARLAND

Start amassing pieces of scrap paper – most types can be used to make these beads as long as they are brightly colored. Thick paper will make heavy, bulky beads, and thinner paper will make more refined and delicate beads.

Ingredients

2yd (1.8m) colored cord

Selection of colored papers, 18 x 13¾in (45 x 35cm)

◆ EQUIPMENT ◆

Craft glue

Paintbrush

3 garden stakes, 20in (50cm) long

Sharp knife

1 Brush craft glue onto the reverse of one piece of colored paper, leaving about 3in (7.5cm) at the bottom without any glue.

2 Lay the stake across the end of the unpasted section of paper and roll the paper tightly around it. When you reach the end of the paper, leave the stake in place while the glue dries to prevent warping. Repeat with the other sheets of colored paper.

3 When the glue is dry, use a sharp knife to slice the paper tube into 1in (2.5cm) beads. Leave the stake in place while slicing to prevent the beads from being squashed in the process.

4 Measure out a piece of cord as long as you want the garland to be. Thread the beads onto it one by one, tying the string in a loop around the bead at each end of the garland to secure.

TOPIARY TREES

COLLECT A CLUSTER of miniature topiary trees in varying shapes and colors for an original Christmas display. A tiny conical evergreen topped with a majestic purple bauble mimics a Christmas tree, while a larger ball of holly and berried ivy sits on top of deliciously scented cinnamon sticks. Dried hydrangea heads, gold balls, and pink paper flowers make a lasting arrangement that contrasts well with the glossy density of evergreens.

MAKING A TOPIARY TREE

Ingredients

Block florist's
foam, 13½ x 4 x 3⅛in
(34 x 10 x 8cm)

Pot, 5½in
(14cm) tall

10in (25cm)
bamboo stick

4 branches
boxwood

Small
bauble

◆ EQUIPMENT ◆

Kitchen knife

1 floral wire
(medium gauge)

Boxwood sprigs
pushed together
to hide foam

Flat square surface
for bauble at top
of pyramid

1 Cut a block of florist's foam into two pieces, each 4 x 4 x 3¼in (10 x 10 x 8cm). Place one on top of the other and push the bamboo stick through both of them. Use a kitchen knife to cut the foam into a four-sided pyramid, leaving a small flat surface at the top.

2 Cut the remaining foam to fit the pot, and put it inside. Set the pyramid on top, using the bamboo stick to secure.

3 Break the branches of boxwood into tiny sprigs and, starting at the bottom, push them one by one into the foam pyramid so no foam shows.

4 Gradually build up the boxwood sprigs until the foam is completely covered. To finish, slip a wire through the loop on the bauble and push it into the flat surface of foam at the top.

HOLLY AND IVY SPHERE
Stand a bunch of long cinnamon sticks in a pot filled with dry florist's foam, and push a ball of damp florist's foam covered in sprigs of holly and berried ivy onto the cinnamon sticks. Cover the filled pot with a layer of velvety bun moss and decorate with a gold star and a scattering of tiny gifts.

PRETTY IN PINK
Push dried hydrangea heads, paper roses and gold papier-mâché balls on wires into dry florist's foam and wedge it into a pot. Finish with a lavish bow.

Cinnamon sticks act as a stem

*T*o a child every Christmas tree is a beautiful and silent sentry keeping steadfast watch over the family's seasonal treasures.

MINI TREE
Contrast shiny evergreen leaves with purple and matte gold for a regal look.

Acknowledgments

C.R.Gibson®
FINE GIFTS SINCE 1870

This book is based on *Ultimate Christmas*, first published in Great Britain in 1996
by Dorling Kindersley Limited, London

Copyright © 2000 Dorling Kindersley Limited, London
Ultimate Christmas text copyright © 1996 Jane Newdick

All rights reserved under International and Pan-American Copyright
Conventions. No part of this publication may be reproduced, stored
in an retrieval system, or transmitted in any form or by any means,
electronic, mechanical, photocopying, recording or otherwise,
without the prior written permission of the copyright owner.

Developed by Matthew A. Price, Nashville, Tennessee.

Published by C. R. Gibson®
C. R. Gibson® is a registered trademark of Thomas Nelson, Inc.
Norwalk, Connecticut 06856

Printed in China by South China Printing

ISBN 0–7667–6759–0
UPC 082272–46689–0
GB4156

Picture Credits

Photography by Dave King